Wisdom

The Principle Thing: Get It!

by William Owens

WISDOM: THE PRINCIPLE THING - GET IT!
Copyright 1996 © William Owens
email: william@throughpeople.com

Scripture quotations are taken from the
Holy Bible, King James Version

Published by:
Through People
Elk Grove, CA
www.throughpeople.com

ISBN: 0-9658629-1-7
Printed in the United States of America!

Introduction

You are about to be exposed to a few words that will impact you one way or the other. This is not a book that was written to make friends (Though I believe it will). It is not meant to make the young person fit in with what is right through trying to make what is right look fun and easy. Nor will it be religiously correct in condoning certain activity that is in the church, which has done much to only lower the standard of God's Kingdom. His Kingdom requirements are no less for young people than they are for everybody. The body count in Hell is rising and the young person occupies much of it. Only the truth exposed through the words of wisdom will deliver young and old from evil.

Make no mistake there is a generation of young people who are full of God's wisdom. They have yielded their lives to the power of God's word and have not bowed the knee to this world. This book is designed to drive you to decide. To choose life or death. Right or wrong. Light or darkness. To be a fool or to be wise. It's written to make you face the reality of consequences that will follow your every decision; both good and bad. It's written to get you uncomfortable with following the crowd and help you get secure into what life is all about. Wisdom is really all that matters. You either have it or you don't.

All I have to offer you are a few words about the power of wisdom that can revolutionize your life. If you simply yield and consider the words of Proverbs chapter 8, you will be astounded at the reality of the words and how they apply to your very life. You are young and the decisions that you about to make will determine your future. It will determine the future of your spouse to be and the children that you will have one day. Wisdom can solve a lot of your problems. Wisdom can save you a life-style of heart ache and above all wisdom will preserver you and keep you for the purpose for which you where made.

The only friend you really have is wisdom. Shhh... Can you hear....? Wisdom is speaking even now. Are you listening?

William Owens
May 2003

Wisdom

THE PRINCIPLE THING:

GET IT!

Pro 8:1 Does not wisdom call out? Does not understanding raise her voice?

The question is clear and the excuses are all swept away. It's very important that as a young man or young woman, you understand that this above question is being asked. Think about it. When you are deciding to do something that is questionable or that you know is not right, don't you hear a voice saying, "No"? Or perhaps you feel a bit uncomfortable doing it. This is wisdom calling out!

When it appears that the circumstances surrounding you would insist that you must do it this way, or when your friends or even your loved ones would persuade you to do it their way, you still can hear a voice saying not to do it and why. This is understanding.

Throughout your life, the voice of wisdom calling out and understanding putting forth her voice will be determined by you yielding to them more and more. The reason why so many young people are not paying attention to these voices that God has placed in their conscious is because they ignore these voices at a young age. God wants you to listen to these voices while you are young. If you do you will develop a hearing ear that grow stronger as you mature into adulthood.

Notes

_____
_____
_____
_____
_____
_____
_____
_____
_____
_____
_____

Wisdom:

There are many voices or persuasions that come from the flesh, from the devil, and even from other people and do not come from wisdom or understanding. This is how you can quickly identify those people whose lives are either in trouble, or going to be in trouble.

To determine whether or not you want to associate with a person try asking them when was the last time they listened to wisdom or when they paid attention to the voice of understanding. It's not enough for young men to get together and just discuss the mistakes they made and then try to justify those mistakes. As a young lady, you can't justify yourself with simple reasoning. You have go to learn to listen to wisdom and apply understanding. They will keep you from repeating the same mistakes over and over again.

APPLICATION

In order for wisdom to be heard in your life on a daily basis, your spirit must be born again. Ask Jesus to come into your life and forgive you of your sins, and to teach you wisdom and give you understanding. However do not confuse this with religion. This is about relationship. You must understand that not only does He become your Savior, but also becomes your Lord.

It's important that you do not confuse becoming a Christian with becoming a member of a social club or something popular. In fact you can not "just become a

Notes

_____
_____
_____
_____
_____
_____
_____
_____
_____
_____
_____

Christian". God calls you to His Son, not a man. You will know if your salvation is a genuine work of God by His Spirit, or a work of religion by men.

Pro 8:2 On the heights along the way, where the paths meet, she takes her stand;

Despite all the confusion that might exist in your life as a young man, wisdom is speaking out. Wisdom is calling out. She is doing her best to obtain your undivided attention. This is a fact and you cannot make excuses for it. You cannot play dumb and just shrug your shoulders as if you didn't know. In other words, if bad happens, you can no longer say, "It's not my fault. I didn't know." Wisdom is trying to let you know. Are you blowing her off?

She is on the highest place in the city, and at the crossroads of every turn. She is at the point of every decision, saying to you what is right. All you have to do is listen. Just take the time to listen. You are listening to your own wit and are making more trouble for yourself. You are listening to the advice of others and no one seems to really know how to instruct you the way you need it. Wisdom knows you. She is aware of your every situation. She even knows the people involved in the decisions you are making better than you, or even they know themselves.

Notes

_____
_____
_____
_____
_____
_____
_____
_____
_____
_____

Late night talk shows, psychics and even some of the sit-coms that attempt to reflect answers to lifes challenges, are not answers to <u>real</u> life. They offer humanistic or self-help alternatives that are built upon the ability of self or even lies that are inspired by satan. Truth is wisdom speaking a knowledge to you that is based on peace, love, and righteousness, and not lies based on the deceptiveness of the human heart that is motivated by greed, self and power.

Look up! Wisdom is standing in the path. She is at the height of where you are walking. Listen to her voice. She is very aware of your hurts and has the healing you need. All you need is the willingness to respond to the insights given through relationship with Jesus Christ. Wisdom always points you to a Savior and there is only one Savior. His name is Jesus, the Only Begotten Son of God, Who died for your sins. Yes, your sins! It's your sins that have you in so much trouble. You didn't do it; you and I were born into sin. But wisdom has the answer. Look up!

Notes

_____
_____
_____
_____
_____
_____
_____
_____
_____
_____
_____

APPLICATION:

Whatever is taking place in your life, whether good or bad, you must always keep your view on wisdom for moment by moment direction and guidance. Wisdom will never speak of itself, but will always point you to your Creator and toward decisions which bring life, not death. Just use this as a simple rule. Does your decision give you the right to just pretty much do what you want to do? Does your decision take the other person's feelings in consideration? Does your decision protect life and values, or does it *act like* it protects life and values? If your decisions are nothing more than a cover-up, you need to get real. Get wisdom.

Pro 8:3 beside the gates leading into the city, at the entrances, she cries aloud:

How much more does this show that wisdom wants to be so involved in your life? Get a clue. Wake up! Get real. What more could a human in their right mind want than the supreme insights of God calling unto them? Don't confuse this voice with mere philosophy or deceptive forms of so called wisdom that is void of power to keep you from an immoral life-style.

Notes

She is crying out at the gates. The gates. The entry points of serious issues in life. At the entrance of the city. We always think that the city life is the way to go. We say, "If I could only make it in the city, I would have it made!" Think again. Wisdom is at the entry of this so called city. She is there to reveal to you the truth of the city and its dangers. She is warning you of those lights which glitter, but bring only pain, not pleasure. Oh, yes. It feels good for a season, for a moment, but then the end is bitter. So bitter.

It's amazing at the caution we feel when we are heading into areas that are dangerous. We just don't feel it for nothing. Young man. Young woman. That's wisdom saying, "Don't. Stop!" Danger". Wisdom is trying to protect you from the dangers of the flesh, from the plight of the wicked, and from a life of difficulty that lies ahead because of a few minutes of pleasure today.

She is at the coming in at the doors speaking to you and you think you are talking to yourself. She is that voice that you heard when you say, "Something told me not to do that!" You've got to get a grip and obey what is right and true because if you do, you benefit. If you don't, you suffer. Yeah, you're right. It's your life. You can do what you want. You are absolutely right. You can. But know this - that as you come in at the doors of life, if you ignore the truth, you will suffer, you will hurt, and you will pay the price.

APPLICATION:

Listen. God loves you, and when His Son Jesus died on the cross, though it might sound kind of wild, He was thinking about you. You don't have to understand it; just believe it. At every entry point of your life, wisdom is crying out to let you know that you don't have to experiment in your life. There are definites that you can build your life on. There are things that are certain to work, but you have to make a commitment. The commitment you make is not to some religion, church, pastor. You make that commitment to the Man Jesus Christ and He will make a commitment to you. A commitment you can feel. But more than just feel, a commitment that you can

Notes

_____
_____
_____
_____
_____
_____
_____
_____
_____
_____
_____

see happening. He is with you. He is not dead. He just doesn't give you some words He left behind. He has given you Himself and His power to walk in authority. Not to be a victim. Only through Jesus Christ do you really have the power to, "Just Say NO". She's crying....listen.

Pro 8:4 "To you, O men, I call out; I raise my voice to all mankind.

Wisdom is not simply calling out to all of creation; she is calling out to the human race. To you, young man who is considering using drugs, or to you young lady considering giving up your precious virginity for a guy you think loves you and is such a hunk. Both of you need to wake up! Your bodies are precious in God's sight. You only have one chance to give up your precious blood to drugs, and your precious body to a sexual relationship that is outside of a lifetime commitment!

Notes

Who are you listening to? What is their life like. Take a close look. Will they be there when it doesn't work out the way they predicted? This is not a movie. Take off the 3-D glasses. Those people who play those sexy roles are being paid to make it look real. You ought to see the problems they have for being paid to be someone they are not!

She is raising her voice to all mankind. Black, white, yellow, Oriental, and even those who are a combination of God's nationalities. Stop being prejudiced against the one who has a different shade of skin, or a unique background. You both could like the same things, and probably even like each other if you would just chat for a minute. Besides if everyone was one color people would then determine their nationalities by the color of their eyes! In other words, it's not our skin, it's our fear. We fear what we are not comfortable with. Wisdom teaches us different.

Notes

_____

_____

_____

_____

_____

_____

_____

_____

_____

_____

_____

She raises her voice to call out the decrees of God that are designed to insure that you live and not die; overcome and not be overcome. She beckons that you may arise to the beauty of life and not be crumbled under the many pitfalls that are awaiting your uninformed decision. That's what it is - uninformed. You don't have the proper information. I truly believe most people who make the wrong decisions in life don't do it intentionally. They are misinformed and don't even know it. Some are given information that is destructive and think they have the whole truth. This goes for those who are in the church as well. Just because they have a bible doesn't mean they are telling the truth.

The devil used the scriptures to attempt to deceive Jesus. You have got to have a personal, proactive, day by day relationship with God through Jesus Christ <u>yourself</u>.

The Principle Thing: Get It!

The voice is being raised and the only way you will hear it is that you want to hear it and that you seek to hear it every day of your life. You will choose the way that is narrow. Your friends will be few because they will want the way of sensuality and pleasure. So what, these are not friends, their fools. While on the onset it seems that all is well with that kind of life, in the end, they will regret the choices they made. You, however, will be growing in true life through a real relationship with Jesus Christ. Not a shallow, "I'm a Christian, I go to church" type of religious talk, but a walk that is different from the world, from your friends, and from a form of godliness that has no power!

And please do not be satisfied to comfort yourself with anything from the world with the weak excuse that you are young. With all due respect, no church, pastor or bishop has the right to interpret God's holiness for God. He said be ye separate from the world, do not love the world or the things in the world. And how man still wants to condone some aspect of the world. It will not work. You will stay true to one or the other, but not both. Would you expect your wife or husband to have an occasional affair with a stranger? Then why do you expect God to allow you to have one? I know you have your arguments, but be sure you have scripture as well as the character of God ways and nature to support it.

Notes

_____
_____
_____
_____
_____
_____
_____
_____
_____
_____
_____
_____

Wisdom:

No man can serve two masters: for either he will hate the one, and love the other; or else he will hold to the one, and despise the other. Ye cannot serve God and mammon.   Matthew 6:24

APPLICATION:

If you and I are listening to wisdom through relationship with Jesus Christ, it will go beyond our lips and produce fruit in our life-style. If a person's religion doesn't affect their morals, then their religion is sick. Smell the bacon and wake up. The year is 2003. We're at war again, people are getting sick from all sorts of viruses and plagues and it's not getting better. It's not enough to simply rest in your self righteousness and think you can get by. God wants you to walk with Him, so if death calls for you, your walk with Him will not be interrupted, but you will step right into glory.

Notes
_____
_____
_____
_____
_____
_____
_____
_____
_____
_____
_____
_____

Pro 8:5 You who are simple, gain prudence; you who are foolish, gain understanding.

It's amazing at the number of simple minded people that exist in a square mile. I'm not trying to sound like I have all the answers, nor do I want to downgrade any person. But if we give an honest assessment of this fact, people have *chosen* to be simple by ignoring wisdom. Thousands, even millions, have chosen the quick and easy way. Instant grits, "lunch in 10 minutes or it's free", delivery with a guarantee, love without pain, sex without consequences. These are simple solutions (so they think) for men and women who have developed their own rule of life. Many are dead for doing it their way. Dead from sickness, disease, or even from purposelessness. Maybe they live a long life, but that doesn't mean it was a whole, complete, and fulfilling life.

Prudence must be gained. Anything that is worth having will come through labor, and the mysteries of life are no different. Another thought for prudence is reason, common sense, shrewdness, insights. We all were born in sin. Yes, in sin. Don't let this surprise you, and don't pride yourself into believing that you were born perfect. Look around. The problem is not the Congress, the whites, the blacks, Japan, or California. The problem is the heart. It's sick and the vital signs indicate...SIN! Sin means unable to do what is right even if you tried. It means missing the mark. It is a nature problem not a will problem. A pig has the nature to want to be in mud. Even if it agreed that it was messy, it is in its nature so eventually the nature will win out.

Notes

When you accept Christ as your Lord and Savior, He changes your nature. He gives you a new nature, a divine nature and that nature wants to walk in the light with God, not in darkness. You have to feed this new nature. One of the main courses of this divine diet is that of wisdom. As you do many of the things you do now, you will not want to do. Because your will has changed to that of your new nature!

Don't buy that escapism idea that you're not a sinner. If you don't think you are in sin, then you won't ever seek to gain prudence. You will always be simple, and the results of your life will show you a fool. Notice I said, the *results*. Results don't lie. While some of you think you have results, keep living. Even weeds take time to grow, and if you have chosen the simple routes in life, the path might seem green and beautiful, but the end of your trip will blow you away. Those breath taking trees and that green grass are props. You are in the desert. Just take a closer look. Your decisions are based on you, your feelings, your desires, or even your hurts. Get real and get free.

Notes

_____
_____
_____
_____
_____
_____
_____
_____
_____
_____
_____

Foolishness is a result of being simple, and the lack of prudence or reason will result in being without simple understanding. While it's expected that a high school graduate would understand simple arithmetic, likewise, should the normal competent adult have understanding. But many don't. Someone can teach you math, but only God can teach you prudence and understanding. If it is good, it comes from God. There is no good thing within man. This might be difficult for you to accept, because of the free-thought that is so prevalent to day. But it is the Word of God.

The Principle Thing: Get It!

Ro 7:18 For I know that in me (that is, in my flesh,) dwelleth no good thing: for to will is present with me; but how to perform that which is good I find not.

Stupidity is a result of a continual ignoring of God and His counsel. Many people, regardless of their natural accomplishments, are stupid. This includes doctors, lawyers, preachers, politicians, professional athletes, movie stars and every person who has not and does not sit in the counsel of the Lord. Money does not make you wise - it simply gives you the ability to be who you are in a more obvious way. A fool would spend foolishly while a wise person would spend wisely.

I challenge you, young person, to talk to the Lord about His wisdom. Ask Him for understanding. He will give His understanding and you will know that it comes from Him and not man. This is imparted to the real you. It is not learned in your mind. The real you is your spirit. You must be born again to hear prudence and gain unlimited understanding. Listen, live, arise, be free, be real and above all be holy through the new nature that is in you, not of your own self or own strength. You can be holy because your new nature IS holy.

Notes

APPLICATION:

Only when one admits they lack, can they truly begin to gain. In order to gain prudence, you must admit you have a lack. Your lack is first of all a personal Savior that has committed Himself to your salvation. Think about it. We all have to worship someone or something bigger than ourselves. For those who think, "Bang! and it happened" (the Big Bang theory), so do I.... God spoke and, BANG! it happened. Listen. God made you in such a way that you are wired to want Him. You want God like a Southerner wants fried chicken, like a duck wants water, like a bee wants honey, like a baby wants its mother's breast, like a man wants to love, like a woman wants to be loved, like a son wants a father, and newlyweds want a honeymoon. We've been fixed by God to want Him and when we refuse Him, we simply create our own god which is nothing more than ourselves doing what we want to do the way we want to do it.

Notes

_____
_____
_____
_____
_____
_____
_____
_____
_____
_____
_____

Jesus said, "*I am the way, the truth, and the life: no man cometh unto the Father, but by me*" (John 14:6). Jesus is the way to the Father, because Jesus is the only One Who died to justify your sins before a Holy God. Yes, you black man. God knows where you are and from whence you've come. Stop trying to go back to your motherland, because no one comes from their mother; the seed comes from the father. God is your father and He has sent His Son to reclaim and redeem you because you were in Him before you were in Africa, before you, white man, were in England, Jamaica, Switzerland, California, Japan or any other location of God's footstool.

Repent and rest. Cease from your own labors which bring no life. Come unto Jesus as you are and He shall make all things brand new. Be simple no more.

Pro 8:6 Listen, for I have worthy things to say; I open my lips to speak what is right.

Let us establish on the onset that wisdom has some worthy things to express, some things that are worth listening to. It's amazing how ready we are to give a ready ear to people we don't know. We dial a 900 # and are prepared to pay $3 per minute for someone to make us feel like we are going the right way, or we receive this new profound direction they give us based on some cardboard boxes that's been shaped into cards which simply provide a medium for satan to work his deception through. Just consider this, that if the majority of what you heard was true, why is there so much trouble in our world? The reason is obvious; the majority of what you hear is a lie! That explains why people have so many problems and our world is passing away.

Wisdom, however, will open her mouth and speak what is right. If there is one thing you and I need, that is

Notes

_____

_____

_____

_____

_____

_____

_____

_____

_____

_____

_____

proven, tested, and rock hard facts which are based on the power of God. Only wisdom can speak that to you and in your spirit through Jesus Christ the Lord.

People are seeking solutions to serious life long problems that go back prior to their birth. The generation before them had the problem, and now they have it. Quite naturally, their children are doomed to have it. The psychiatrist has more problems than you, and has yet to produce a proven track record in bringing forth the right answer. There is merely a shifting of the reasons for things. You can read many books on religion, metaphysics, science of the mind, or think your breathing techniques will manifest some sort of divine inspiration. When it's all said and done, however, you will come up with the same old worn out deception which says, "You are experiencing your life for yourself, and are going through what you must go through. In the end, you will be a better person and have a stronger mind. You must press past the pain and get in contact with your true self. Only then, will you discover the beauty of life and all that it has to offer you. Be kind to yourself and do what is in your heart to do. Only believe. All will be fine". Lies and deception from the pit of hell.

Notes

_____
_____
_____
_____
_____
_____
_____
_____
_____
_____
_____

Doesn't it all sound so considerate and profoundly simple? But when you really look into this form of reasoning, it can be summed up in one word; ESCAPISM.

There is not one definite in this form of wisdom. There is no responsibility for ones choices in it. It is all built upon an appeal to simply keep on keeping on and eventually it will all work out. The wisdom of God has a better offer through His Son Jesus Christ. It has *assured* you that right things will come out of her mouth. That means that you might not like it, but it will be right. It means it might not be popular, but it will bring about life and not death. It means that if you would listen and make this the center of your life, you will hear worthy and right things all the days of your life. Without a doubt, you will be blessed, assured, confident and have real hope.

APPLICATION:

Regardless of how fun your life might be right now as a young person, I challenge you to set aside the idea that shallowness will bring about good. Don't attempt to find peace by avoiding being serious. AIDS is serious, sex is serious, death is serious, life is serious, God is serious and HELL is serious. So why do you avoid being serious about life that is full of serious consequences? I could see if the consequences were fake, but they're not. Neither should you be.

Wisdom will speak what is right to you in every situation. You can be assured that if you would apply these truths, wisdom will speak to your heart through

Notes

_____
_____
_____
_____
_____
_____
_____
_____
_____
_____
_____

Wisdom:

Jesus Christ. You will see and perceive a difference about yourself, about others, and about the future. Ask the Lord Jesus Christ into your heart today. Simply pray this prayer from your heart:

"Lord, come into my life. I repent of my sins and I commit my life to you. Protect me from the many lies that are prevalent. I have chosen to listen and hear what is right. I confess that Jesus is Lord. I believe He rose from the dead and that my spirit is born again. I am a new creation. Amen".

Pro 8:7 My mouth speaks what is true, for my lips detest wickedness.

Whenever truth is spoken, wickedness is revealed as well. As a young person, you are being constantly bombarded with what is wicked and very seldom come in contact with the truth. From the time you wake up and listen to your music, until the time your day ends, you are experiencing a form of life that is not true. That slow jam that puts you into a frame of mind to want to do what the lyrics say makes it sound so easy. Shouldn't you consider that perhaps what you are listening to is not true? Take a closer look at that beer commercial. Notice that weekly show that you just have to see and really listen to what they are laughing about. Is it true, or is it wicked?

Don't get so uncomfortable when I use the word wicked. Call a spade a spade, and call wicked- wicked Remember,

Notes

_____
_____
_____
_____
_____
_____
_____
_____
_____
_____

most of the things you see advertised in magazines, on television, and on radio, is presented to offer you happiness. It's presented to offer an answer to your loneliness and rejection. It wants you to buy its remedy for whatever your problem might be, but it *doesn't offer you the truth!*

There is a source, however, that you can trust in. That is the wisdom of God through Jesus Christ the Lord. You can put your total life in His hands knowing that He is aware of how you feel. He is in touch with who you are and He doesn't cater to your weaknesses. Rather, He delivers you from them! How different Jesus is from everyone else. These so called gods *never* offer to bring you out of your problems. Instead, they simply offer to adjust the bondage to show you how to live with it and to try to make it right. But they never give you power over your problems because they have no power. They have no power because they do not exist. Do not let your "issues" become nothing more than a self willed excuse permitted to dictate your life decisions or render you enabled to decide at all.

Notes

Wisdom will speak what is right because wickedness is detestable to her lips. This gives you an assurance that as you walk with God, He will always speak truth to you. As well, those who will come close to you will speak the same thing. If they don't, you will know that they don't mean well and only want you for themselves. Open thine eyes and see. Cut that music off and listen to the music of truth. You can still dance, but your dance will be to a new beat and to a holy rhythm. Amen.

APPLICATION:

You have got to do something about this area of your life. You can't just buy into everything and everyone that is talking to you. The spirit of this age wants you to become victim to its allurements and only through allowing wisdom to speak to you, will you know what is true.

Notes
_____
_____
_____
_____
_____
_____
_____
_____
_____
_____
_____

Begin to take the time to apply what you have read and test the things that you believe. If you are unwilling to test them, then you are afraid of being wrong. If you are afraid of being wrong, then more than likely you are. When you walk with wisdom, you might not understand everything you believe, but you have a confidence to stand. You have a boldness of a lion and you have a life to show that what you believe has power. Power separates those whose gods have been manufactured by their own hands from the God Who made us with His own hands.

You can feel that in your gut that what is being said is true. Why? Because you were wired by God for God and He is calling you home. Come on. He has prepared a table for you and it's time that you don't make any more excuses. Besides, you have friends that are waiting to get to know you. Go to church this Sunday. You'll see.

Pro 8:8 All the words of my mouth are just; none of them is crooked or perverse.

How many times do we consider if one is telling us the truth? When we listen, we do so attempting to discern if there is a possibility of deceit in ones motives. In every area of life, we are listening or we are speaking. Always, either of two things are being said; truth or lie. We depend upon loved ones to direct us in a way that will insure our best interest. We even look to athletes, movie stars, recording artists, and other visible personalities to try to obtain some sort of word that we can put our life on. In the end, we find perversion and some form of information that is biased or outright wrong. But we pay the price. We suffer at the words of the mouths of people who are unable to speak what we need to know.

Notes

To be perfectly honest with you, no one can give you the exact words for you but the One who made you. The most upright person can speak 1 million words of some of the most wisest sayings, and you will still be in need of another word for another day to keep on living. Another persons security will never do for your own security. As well, your lack of

Wisdom:

insecurity makes you a prey for many abusers in the world. There is a better way.

All the words of wisdom are just and none of them are twisted or lawless. As you walk with God through His Son Jesus Christ, you will be the pupil of wisdom day in and day out. You will have direct and continual access to wisdom for your every decision. At times, even when you are not sure what to do and the answer is not there immediately, you will have confidence to just stand and let God work it out according to His righteousness for good. Your good. Jesus is not an asterisk. He is not a far fetched religious idea. He is a person. He is real. He really died, was buried, and rose from the grave. He is not a figment of the imagination of millions of people who have put their trust in Him. If the story of Jesus was a lie, there would be no way it could survive this long and change the lives of young people just like you who decided to give their souls to Him and only Him. When you do, just like millions of others, you will know peace and you will be led by wisdom and hear words that are not just crooked and perverse.

Notes

_____
_____
_____
_____
_____
_____
_____
_____
_____
_____
_____

APPLICATION:

You can listen to wisdom one day and then listen next week. You can practice your flute one day, then next week. But only when you practice that flute everyday will you become effective and consistent at being good. In the same way, you have to spend time with God your Father through Jesus Christ your Lord and wisdom will speak to you and guide your life in accordance with God's purpose for making you. You are not a mistake. The words that will precede out of the mouth of wisdom will speak this truth to you.

In order to retain this wisdom, you must refrain from those things that are contrary to sound wisdom such as music, movies and partying because these elements have their own philosophy which is based on pleasure and not life. God will show you how to have fun in ways you never dreamed of. He will show you how to laugh without taking away life and sacrificing values. How to love without sex, and how to be a part of a party that's eternal and not temporal. Everything in the arts was created by God and the world, through satan, has perverted it. Apply this truth and you will begin to see the beauty in everything around you. Fear no more.

Notes

_____
_____
_____
_____
_____
_____
_____
_____
_____
_____
_____

Pro 8:9 To the discerning all of them are right; they are faultless to those who have knowledge.

The reason why a fool cannot comprehend wisdom is because they have not learned to discern wisdom. You see, wisdom is not wisdom to everyone. Wisdom is a language that you have to be taught just like any other language. As you discern English or Spanish, so must you learn to discern wisdom. As you do, you will come to know that her words are just and right. This is why you have to *continue* to apply yourself because as you do so, your discernment will increase and you will be able to tell truth from error. Inconsistency is the greatest threat to any form of growth. Your soul's enemy will gain his victory through a lack of growing in a discerning knowledge.

Notes

_____
_____
_____
_____
_____
_____
_____
_____
_____
_____

The reason they are faultless or without error to those who have knowledge is because they have seen the results of wisdom work in their life. The reason why millions are so committed to Jesus Christ is because there is a difference. They are changed. They have been set free from the things that would control them. From sex, drugs and the simple ideas about life that are false. Urges that seem uncontrollable, to a peace and a soberness that human ability cannot give. These are words that have spoken the world into existence therefore such power is limitless to accomplish your total freedom.

You would be surprised at how many people find fault with wisdom. Even those who mean well. You know why? Because wisdom does not appeal to the flesh. As a result, everyone limits themselves in some way to its instruction. Yet the more we grow in knowledge, the more we come to know that wisdom is right it all of her ways.

God's grace is so important because we are allowed to walk where we are and not try to grow up overnight. Don't be discouraged from coming to God because you think you're no good. You're right. No one is any good, for if we could be good before we come to Him, then why come to Him at all? Come as you are and listen to the faultless words of wisdom.

APPLICATION:

Be free to consciously apply the discernment of what wisdom is teaching you, and you will discover that wisdom is right. Remember, wisdom speaks through the pages of the bible by the spirit of Jesus Christ, not through chance with an abstract thought. Dedicate yourself to spending time everyday in God's word, and you will perceive the knowledge coming forth with power!

Notes

Pro 8:10 Choose my instruction instead of silver, knowledge rather than choice gold,

It appears that the bottom line in life is money. Get it. Keep it. Spend it. Don't let anything threaten your financial position and possibilities. The rich get richer and the poor yet struggle. Our society is divided over money and as a young person, you will have to deal with the motive of money all your life. You don't have any problem buying just what you want, regardless of how expensive it is because it establishes your identity with yourself and with others. But you need money to

Wisdom:

do it. So you set yourself to find out how you will get those $150 shoes, or that $325 official jacket. And girl, don't forget those jeans. You know you got to have it. Before you know it, you are caught up in the fury of working to spend and your life takes shape over the outer things rather than the inner things. As a result, money is the order of the day because without money, you don't get your identity, and without identity you have no sense of being, no friends, no hope. WAKE UP!

Notes

_____
_____
_____
_____
_____
_____
_____
_____
_____
_____
_____

Wisdom is saying to choose her instruction instead of silver because without her insights, silver would be spent on vain things and would still be unable to impart life to your true self which is your spirit. When you look around you and see the rich spend their money, they spend it on things that only cover up the pain. They spend it on items that make them look happy. Yeah, Mr. Cool, that $30,000 dollar car can make you *look* successful, that designer suit, Ms. Vogue can make you *look* like you have "arrived". But when these same people open their mouths, what comes out? Foolishness. Shallowness. Vain conversation. Your wealth is determined by who you are without money because money might make you rich, but only instruction and knowledge can make you wealthy.

APPLICATION:

The next time you are challenged to make a decision about money or wisdom, really sit down and think what the pros and cons are for both of them. Get a piece of paper and draw a line down the middle and look at the benefits of them both. Think about the long term effects of choosing wisdom and the character that you will be building. Think about the type of friends you will choose because of this and the type of wife or husband you will make because of choosing instruction and knowledge over temporary pleasures that money can bring. But then, think about it when wealth is brought to you and how you will possess the money, and it won't posses you. Take your time and build the wealth that will last through Jesus Christ the Lord.

Pro 8:11 for wisdom is more precious than rubies, and nothing you desire can compare with her.

Why should you have more desire for instruction and knowledge in your younger years than that of mere silver and gold? Because she is more precious that the revenues, the appearance, and the lasting value of silver and gold. Once you come into a commitment with God through Jesus Christ, you will come to realize that nothing that you could ever desire could be compared with her.

Notes

_____
_____
_____
_____
_____
_____
_____
_____
_____
_____
_____

Wisdom:

I mean, I can desire a lot of things. A 65 ft. modernized yacht with the latest in technology and design. Fully furnished in European style furnishing, complete with a full crew prepared to go at all times, capable of staying on the waters for months and traveling the full length of any trip. Or how about a 15 room mansion, located on the tranquil islands of the Tropics with ivory throughout and furnishings specifically designed as an original? This sits on the beach with the water only a few feet away from your own salt free swimming pool and outdoor garden. The price tag exceeds 9 million, and maintenance is about $200,000 per year. The list could be endless. Clothes, automobiles, trips around the world, pretty women, handsome men, food, sex, fun, pleasures and yet nothing you desire can be compared with wisdom.

Notes

_____

_____

_____

_____

_____

_____

_____

_____

_____

_____

_____

How could this be? Remember, you are created in God's image. You were wired for God to abide in you. You were not created for things; they were created for you. You could never be fulfilled in your spirit by a boat, by a car, by clothes, by sex, but only by God. You can get in a boat, but it can't get in you. You can drive a car, but it can't drive you. You can put clothes on but they can't put you on. You can travel around the world, but the world could not travel around your lonely heart and soul.

But once you taste the goodness of the Lord and His wisdom, your soul rejoices, your heart flutters, your mind finds peace, your spirit is released. Why? Because

The Principle Thing: Get It!

Jesus can come inside your spirit because you were wired for Him. He made you in His image and likeness and you will never be fulfilled without Him in your life. Nothing can compare with Him because you are God's special creation designed to be loved by Him and to love Him. What are you waiting for? Reach out to Him and behold, He will reach out to you.

APPLICATION:

Just reflect back in your life a few years and notice what "things" have done for you. Think about it. You couldn't wait to get what you have and the high lasted for a few days, maybe a week, or a month at the most. Now think about the last time you came across wisdom or the peace of God. That experience still has an effect upon you today, and if you have left it, you want it back. Stop being deceived by your fleshly desires as a young person. You don't have to fill your oats young man. Instead, let God fill your heart. You don't have to have sex with that young man to prove you love him, young lady. Let God be your Father and be secure in His love. Be real. Let your desires be for the things which last. All else will come without sorrow if you wait on the Lord.

Notes

Pro 8:12 "I, wisdom, dwell together with prudence; I possess knowledge and discretion.

Who dwells with you? Who do you dwell with? Your

company says a lot about you. It says a lot about your character. It will even reveal what will happen over a period of time in your life, because your dwelling place is where what you believe is actually determined.

As a young person, you spend a lot of time in thought. As you look around your room, your beliefs are expressed right there. Go ahead, look on the walls. What do you see? Look through your music collection, your wardrobe, your clothes. They reflect your dwelling place. Now look especially close to what you read. Thumb through the magazines. Take a close look at what the pictures suggest. Sex, parties, rebellion, independence. Craze. Excessiveness. Violence. What? If these things are in your dwelling place, this answers why you do what you do, why you want what you want, and why you feel the way you feel.

Notes

_____
_____
_____
_____
_____
_____
_____
_____
_____
_____
_____

Wisdom dwells together with prudence. Another way of looking at it is that wisdom has made wise counsel her dwelling. She is saying, "I, wisdom, dwell with insight and experience. I, wisdom, inhabit shrewdness". Do you not realize that you can place wisdom on your walls? Don't you know that your books can reflect experience, and that you can literally posses the power of *true* knowledge (remember that there is a false knowledge) if you simply open yourself up to wisdom *through Jesus Christ the Lord.* This truth will be reflected in how you live, what you desire, and the peace that you will have.

The Principle Thing: Get It!

If I could sell discretion, I would be rich. But would anyone want to buy it? Wisdom not only brings you experience, but also knowledge and discretion. If there is a time when a person needs "know how" in their life and the ability to discern if they should do this or that, it's when they're young. In an age when you are desperately seeking solutions to the issues that face you when you are young and vulnerable, you, young man, and you, young lady, need to become prudent and possess the ability to judge right from wrong.

Don't think that people make mistakes for the fun of it. They don't! Many young people really believe that what they are doing is all right and will work out fine in the end. The next morning, they feel the pain of what they did and there is no going back. The consequences will follow and if one chose wrong, some consequences can be tremendously heavy.

I beg you to stop and check out your dwelling place. Who do you talk on the phone with while you look at that fantasy picture on your wall? You are thinking that you couldn't feel any better and that you know what you are about to involve yourself in is all right. Think again. Come on. Be still for a moment. Listen. Listen. Listen. Wisdom is opening her mouth to speak to you about the very thing you are going through. Close your eyes and ask God to speak to you and to show you truth. God can help you out of your

Notes

_____

_____

_____

_____

_____

_____

_____

_____

_____

_____

Wisdom:

situation. Ask Jesus to come into your life and tell Him you are sorry for your sins and simply want to be free from all the craze. Refuse to be ashamed anymore and see your friends as victims as well.

Make room for wisdom to dwell in your place from this day forward and discretion shall blanket you forever.

Application:

Notes
_____
_____
_____
_____
_____
_____
_____
_____
_____
_____
_____

Whatever steps you need to take to obtain "know how" and the ability to choose right from wrong, take them. The toughest part of any journey is starting. Stop making excuses for what has gone wrong. Stop crying about it and beating yourself up or beating someone else up. Just ask Jesus to come into your life. Old things will pass away and you will be new. In fact, the bible says that He throws your past into the sea of forgetfulness. Repent, Rejoice, and Forget.

Pro 8:13 To fear the LORD is to hate evil; I hate pride and arrogance, evil behavior and perverse speech.

There is a fear that is good. The fear of the Lord is to hate that which God hates. It is to love what God loves. One cannot say they love God and love that which is evil. Can you have two favorites? You are either the fan of one or the other. Any true sports fan will be true to one team and one team only regardless if they are winning or losing. If you expect to be on God's team you will hate the team of evil.

Or consider the small hick town sheriff who would give a ticket to a cockroach for jay walking if it could get it to sign the ticket. We wonder what could be the big deal with jay walking when no cars are in the street. We say what could be the big deal that we must hate evil? If you saw the untimely deaths related to jay walking, you would know why. If you could see the millions of souls lost of lives wrecked by evil, you would hate it as well.

People choose pride because of one reason. The truly believe that they are who they are because of themselves and not because of God. Perhaps you feel so gleeful, young woman, because of your beauty. Young man, you feel invincible because of your shapely body in they gym. Or because of your success. Your fame. Your talent and abilities. Your wit. Your charm. Your your, your. Whatever you are, ask yourself one question. Did you put in there yourself, or did God give it to you? You had better believe you had nothing to do with it. God gave it to you. All you had to do was exercise it and you got better and better.

Notes

_____
_____
_____
_____
_____
_____
_____
_____
_____
_____
_____
_____

Satan chose pride and fell from his first estate in heaven. Your only hope to avoid pride is to hate it. Behind every victory, pride will be there to take it from you. People will be there to stroke you and to pour pride down your throat, but don't take it. Hate it because it will surely bring arrogance. Arrogance is the attitude of pride in action. People who yield to pride think they are better than everyone. They believe that they are above the rest and must show this by an attitude of high-mindedness. In actuality, if they lost their beautiful face, that tremendous talent, that perfect smile, and the quick wit, they would be found humble as a lamb in an instant and wounded beyond the ability to handle it.

Notes

_____
_____
_____
_____
_____
_____
_____
_____
_____
_____
_____

As a young person, don't build your life on such a shallow mask. A fake. A facade. A mirage. Come on, wake up. When matured, all such things combined will bring evil behavior and perverse speech. People just don't start talking any kind of way for nothing. It's an external behavior of an internal condition. You can be locked up, beat up, drugged up, and feared up. But until you are cleaned up in your soul, your behavior is going to be messed up. Keep it simple while you are young. If you master hating evil, regardless of how good it looks, you will be avoiding all the other characteristics that are guaranteed to destroy your life.

APPLICATION:

You have your own world. You're in the decision making years of your life and for the most part, the rule is pretty much, "if it feels good, it's right". Time for a sober wake up call. WRONG! If you are going to choose the way of evil, at least know what kind of life you have coming... heartache after heartache which worsens with time. More importantly, know that you just don't have to choose this form of life. You can say, "Enough is enough. I will choose the way of God from this day forward". Yes, of course the sin and the pleasures of this life *feel* great, but you pay for it. The toll of sin is getting higher and higher, and besides that which appears to be pleasure, it is quickly short lived, for the wages of sin is death. Call out to God for His mercy and ask His Son to come into your life, for in Him resides the power to hate evil. REST.

Notes

Pro 8:14 Counsel and sound judgment are mine; I have understanding and power.

The ownership of counsel and the location of judgment belong to and reside with wisdom. If you hear it from someone else, it's because they obtain it from wisdom. All of the counsel and judgment that is founded upon the earth has originated from wisdom. There is no power or intelligence that is independent of wisdom. Man, in his own ego and vain mind, yet believes that he has within himself the innate ability to decipher the issues of life apart from God. The exclusive ownership of judgment and counsel come from wisdom through relationship with God by Jesus Christ, the RISEN Lord and Savior.

Understanding is needed in every phase of your life. As a young adult entering into many intense times of decision, you need the power of understanding. I truly believe if people had known the outcome, they would have not made that particular decision.

Think about your body. Think about sex and the pleasure that it gives. I mean face it; it feels great! There is nothing like the experience of sex. It is an indescribable part of being human and for the most part, with an exception of a few, people want to have it and will do so at extreme risk. Regardless of how bad you think you have to experiment with your only body by giving up your precious virginity, you need to become intimate with understanding. Even though some have already decided to live a life of "safe sex", you have still missed the whole issue. You need understanding for then you will have strength.

Notes

_____
_____
_____
_____
_____
_____
_____
_____
_____
_____
_____

The reason why people abuse their body and assume that sex is for sex, rather than an expression of love built on a lifetime commitment, is simply because they have not obtained understanding in the person of Jesus Christ. When He gives you this understanding, it's built on love demonstrated in power. When it's all said and done, this is the qualifying issue in your life, in my life, and in every life; POWER. You either have it or you don't. You have the ability to stand against the deceptions of the world, the illusive lie of people, of imaginations, of spirits, of demons, and even of your own rebellious lower nature, or you don't. Come on! Wake up, beloved. God wants to give you love that works by power, and you will see it evident in your everyday life!

APPLICATION:

Get up. Look in the mirror. What do you see? (By the way, you are to really get up and look in the mirror. Thank you). How do you feel? Confident? Ashamed? Scared? Frustrated? Proud? Uncertain? Or, how do you want to feel and what have you done to try to get that feeling?

You have got to remember that you are created in the image of God. You are wired to feel according to God's law. If you are walking in it, you will have a conscience that is void of offense. If you are not, your conscience will condemn you. Or, you are so far gone, you cannot tell a truth from the lie. But you cannot avoid the reality of the conditions that the word of God says. You have counsel, sound judgment, understanding and you walk in power. Or, you don't. You are striving toward God and are found pleasing in His sight without those lame excuses, or you are just doing what you want to do with a nickel or dime excuse that won't hold water on Judgment Day. Apply the test. Look in the mirror. What do you see?

Notes

Pro 8:15 By me kings reign and rulers make laws that are just; 16 by me princes govern, and all nobles who rule on earth.

Wisdom:

Even the kings of the earth, whether they are in Japan, the depths of Africa, Singapore, or the Atlantic, depend upon the inspiration of the Lord to conduct the affairs of their duty. This is without question, whether they believe it or not, whether they call out upon the name of the Lord as Savior, or they think it's by some goodness of their own. God gives the wisdom and ability to perform the given task at hand according to His will which was preordained before the foundation of the earth.

Notes

As a young person, please accept in the depths of your being, that before your mother knew your father, and before the sperm got going to the egg, God knew you. In fact, He saw you before your father fell in love with your mother. For those who don't know your father or perhaps even your mother, whatever your state might be, God yet is aware of you. You could be the result of a rape. It doesn't matter. God knows you, and it is with this same thoroughness that He rules over the affairs of the land, and allows the kings and rulers to make laws that are sent forth to fulfill His mind in the earth among the sons of men.

APPLICATION:

You are attempting to simply live your life. You don't want to hurt anyone, and you don't want anyone to hurt you. You want the hope to love and you want to be loved. Why should such a simple request be so difficult?

Listen, friend. I know you didn't ask to born. I can sympathize with how you might feel, and there are no buts about it. God has a specific plan and purpose for your life. You simply need to get with God through His Son Jesus Christ and you shall know what I say is true. You will find a peace from He who gives wisdom to you, whom He has made a king and a ruler, not over 1 million, not over 1 thousand, not even over 2, simply over 1. That person is you.

Notes

_____
_____
_____
_____
_____
_____
_____
_____
_____
_____
_____

Pr 8:16 By me princes rule, and nobles, even all the judges of the earth.

This truth is without question. Thousands upon thousands of men and women are in constant need of the knowledge necessary to make the right decisions. There is not one person on the earth that is not in need of God's wisdom to rule righteously.

This truth alone should empower you to thrive in depending upon God to give you the wisdom to chose that which would honor Him.

APPLICATION

Seek God with all your passions. Develop the necessary habits of searching out the Lord's quickening to rule and to judge in a way that would show you to be a God fearing man and woman of God. These decisions will follow you all the days of your life and will naturally draw others to you for you to point to Christ who is our wisdom.

Pro 8:17 I love those who love me, and those who seek me find me.

There is a love that can only be given to those who would receive it. A love that demands you pursue it to get it. As a young person, I can imagine the many definitions that you might have of love, or the many more misconceptions that flood your mind and weigh down your spirit.

Notes

_____
_____
_____
_____
_____
_____
_____
_____
_____
_____
_____

Wisdom has the divine ability to love you. And she possesses a divine desire to be loved by you. The invitation has been given by wisdom, but you must receive this blessed opportunity by showing up wherever wisdom will be. What invitation is good when you don't use it? And who would keep sending them if you never showed up?

Wisdom wants you to know that there is no such thing as merely receiving love. In fact, the deepest form of love is to give up your life; to die. Until you are willing to give up your life and die, you will not live. Those who truly live as young people are those who simply give up their lives and walk with God. They are yet human. They make mistakes, yet if they truly love the Lord, they will overcome and come out of that sin.

Pro 8:18 With me are riches and honor, enduring wealth and prosperity.

The human race has always been led to believe that money and fame comes from ourselves whether we are some multi-talented musician, or a one of a kind athlete. The belief is the same. It's within you. You have the power. You can do what you put your mind to do. The bible doesn't support this idealism. It is very clear on where enduring wealth and real prosperity is. It is with wisdom.

Have you wondered why tragedy befalls the stars of our generation or of any generation? Just read the tabloids or watch the news. There is a price they pay for the world's so called "riches and honor".

Think about your life and the plans you have. What dream have you placed your hopes in to give you some money and respect? I challenge you to think again. I don't care what appears to look like it's going to fix you up. If it doesn't come from God's perfect will and relationship with Jesus Christ, it will not last. In fact, you are not even really starting because your life is being based on a temporary idea and not on a solid purpose attached to a person. Don't even think "putting God first" will fix it, because if God is first, really first, then God is also the last of whatever you are doing.

Notes

_____

_____

_____

_____

_____

_____

_____

_____

_____

_____

_____

Wisdom:

And if you are going to live for God, you can't represent this world. He will not share you with another. Base your pursuits upon righteousness, not on assumption, and your wealth and prosperity will endure.

Pro 8:19 My fruit is better than fine gold; what I yield surpasses choice silver.

This is a strong assurance. Wisdom is giving you a promise that it will produce for you! Just think about the many promises certain philosophies have made you. Luck, love, money, and every earthly desire a human could want. However, the wisdom that comes from above through Jesus Christ, promises that its fruit will be better than the choices of gold. Look at how many people wear gold these days. The more the better. The bigger the better and so on. Even silver has been compared to not be able to restore you with the fruit that wisdom will.

Why? Because it's not just about the money. Why do we think if we just had the MONEY, we'd have it made? Come on, think! All you would do is spend it on more of what you're buying now!

Notes

_____
_____
_____
_____
_____
_____
_____
_____
_____
_____
_____

There is a fruit that money can't buy.
Like, money can buy a house
But it can't buy a home.
Money can buy a ring
But it can't buy a marriage.
Money can buy a sex
But it can't buy love.

Money can't buy this kind of fruit and it only comes through obeying the good commandments of God through relationship with Jesus Christ. You can only obey the decrees of God by the Spirit. This is why you must be born again!

Pro 8:20 I walk in the way of righteousness, along the paths of justice,

So, where are you walking? What's the name of the street you are on? Anything Goes? Sex Avenue? Irresponsibility? Violence is My Game? Killed or Be Killed? I Don't Care? Just where are you walking in your life? It will be known by the way you are living! Look at the paths that are adjoined to your street. They reveal the many types of things that can happen to your life.

Notes

_____
_____
_____
_____
_____
_____
_____
_____
_____
_____
_____

If, however, you choose to walk with wisdom you will be in the path of righteousness. Your steps will be ordered of the Lord. You will have an assurance that only God can give. There will be no surprises because God is faithful and will never leave nor forsake you. You see, you've got to dare to believe God regardless of what your friend, your mother, your father, or the world does. Make a bold determination to get a hold of God for yourself and He will place you on the path of the just. The amazing thing about all of this is that you will perceive a peace and a reality that exceeds understanding. In other words, Jesus is the Only God Who can truly provide you with evidence of His reality. He alone has power that is capable of being released in and through you for righteous living that comes through grace.

Pro 8:21 bestowing wealth on those who love me and making their treasuries full.

Society makes God out to be rigid, unfair, boring, and impossible to obey while totally being unrewarding for those who are delightedly attempting to obey His voice and His ways. The bible does not say that! Stop listening to people's opinion's and find out for yourself. You don't believe people when they tell you anything else, so why believe them when they try to tell you about God? Just ask God, through His Son Jesus Christ Who is the only Way, the only Truth and the only Life!

Notes

Wisdom makes a promise to bestow wealth on those who love her. Remember this wealth is not just money. It's more than what money can buy. Your treasures will be filled with those treasures that will endure not just in this life, but in the one to come! Get a grip! Yes, you will live forever in the presence of God or out of His presence. You are an eternal being. The bible says, *"And as it is appointed unto men once to die, but after this the judgment"* Hebrews 9:27. For those who say that you will be reincarnated, ask them to prove it in a document that has withstood the test of time like the bible. They can't! So why believe it? Don't get personal; get factual.

Give your life to Jesus Who is able to fill your treasures with Himself and with all those things that He has purposed for your life!

Pro 8:22 "The LORD brought me forth as the first of his works, before his deeds of old;

Listen, young man, and harken, young woman. Whatever you are believing and basing your life on should be put to the test of not only time, but also by the effect it is having on your life. Wisdom is making a profound statement here. The Lord brought her forth as the first of his works. Whatever you are living, if it is not based on wisdom who is recognized as the first of God's work, what chance do you think you have to succeed?

I mean, really. How and why do people convince themselves that regardless of what God has declared, they are yet going to make it happen? Yeah, right. It doesn't work like that.

The bible tells us why people go on to deceive themselves and others.

Notes

_____
_____
_____
_____
_____
_____
_____
_____
_____
_____
_____

"But if our gospel be hid, it is hid to them that are lost: In whom the god of this world hath blinded the minds of them which believe not, lest the light of the glorious gospel of Christ, who is the image of God, should shine unto them." 2 Corinthians 4:3,4

Wisdom:

This is why people refuse the gospel and why it is so hard for your carnal man to receive it. The devil (satan) wants to blind you from receiving the only truth that can save your soul. Therefore, base your moves on wisdom who was made before you, before me, even before satan who is truly deceiving the world.

Don't live a lie! Your belief should be weighed by your fruit. What does your fruit look like?

Pro 8:23 I was appointed from eternity, from the beginning, before the world began.

Notes

Once again, wisdom goes a step farther and reveals that her appointment was outside of the realm of time. It was from the beginning which shares the title of God, Alpha, meaning "beginning". This correctly correlates with Jesus Who reveals one of His roles to the believer.

"But of him are ye in Christ Jesus, who of God is made unto us wisdom, and righteousness, and sanctification, and redemption: 1 Corinthians 1:30

No one shares in wisdom apart from God. Such wisdom of the earth bears the fruit of the earth. This fruit reveals that its origin is not of God.

"But if ye have bitter envying and strife in your hearts, glory not, and lie not against the truth.
"This wisdom descendeth not from above, but is earthly, sensual, devilish." James 3: 13, 14

All you have to do is be honest with yourself. Behold the fruit that you are believing. What is it producing in yourself as well as in the people who are bringing it to you? Get hooked up to the One Who was appointed before the world, for He is no respecter of persons.

APPLICATION

It only stands to reason that if wisdom has this kind of History with existence, there is no problem in providing you with the insight that you need to overcome in your life. You have to apply this through first believing, then doing. When you are born again, you receive the ability of God by His Spirit and the process begins. Of course it isn't easy. Is walking easy when you begin as a baby? But you do it now without even thinking about it. So likewise as you mature with wisdom, whose beginning was before everything else begun, you will walking with wisdom without thinking about it. It will be like, of course I walk with wisdom, just like, of course I can walk. Cool!

Notes

_____
_____
_____
_____
_____
_____
_____
_____
_____
_____
_____
_____

Pro 8:24 When there were no oceans, I was given birth, when there were no springs abounding with water; 25 before the mountains were settled in place, before the hills, I was given birth, 26 before he made the earth or its fields or any of the dust of the world. 27 I was there when he set the heavens in place, when he marked out the horizon on the face of the deep, 28 when he established the clouds above and fixed securely the fountains of the deep, 29 when he gave the sea its boundary so the waters would not overstep his command, and when he marked out the foundations of the earth. 30 Then I was the craftsman at his side. I was filled with delight day after day, rejoicing always in his presence, 31 rejoicing in his whole world and delighting in mankind.

WOW! AWESOME! This totally places the person who chooses to believe that there is no God without excuses. Yeah, I know you can say, "prove it". To be honest with you, I would waste my time. Because if He doesn't give it to you to believe, then you won't, and you can't.

Notes

_____
_____
_____
_____
_____
_____
_____
_____
_____
_____
_____

Jesus said, "No man can come to me, except the Father which hath sent me draw him: and I will raise him up at the last day." John 6:44

This is what makes God to be God. If He could be placed between your eyes with mere understanding, then why fear Him? Furthermore, why serve Him? God is God, and the bible reveals that before His creation was there, wisdom was.

Look at the power of wisdom's claim. There was absolutely nothing made. No earth, no heaven, no sea, nothing! The same wisdom that would instruct you in the way of living was always with God and is now made available to you. This power will instruct you in the way of excellence. It will protect you from destruction and the way of sin. Wisdom understands every facet of life and is your assurance of being fulfilled, but you have to _choose_ to receive wisdom.

In the complete work that God did, He did something absolutely beyond our conception. He gave you choice. Just imagine that in all of His power, He cannot and will not force His wisdom upon you. Now that's love. The only way He could love you is to let you choose to love Him or reject Him. Now comes the opportunity to receive this profound wisdom.

Pro 8:32 "Now then, my sons, listen to me; blessed are those who keep my ways.

Just what is the conclusion of the whole issue with wisdom? Do you blow wisdom off? Do you harken to her sayings? Do you debate the profound insights to life that God is speaking through wisdom? Do you counteract with some humanistic escape to justify what you want to do? Or do you submit to its truths and conform your life to her sayings and behold the difference that comes upon you, through you, and most importantly to you?

The answer to this question is found in this verse: Listen to ME! Keep MY ways!

Notes

The spirit of Wisdom is so kind and approaches us with such a plea that you really have to deliberately turn your back to her. God has chosen to describe His decrees as wisdom and through wisdom to establish the life of mankind to be blessed. God has made you in His image, and as a result, you have the ability to choose to be for or against His decrees. In all of His power, He asks you

Wisdom:

to listen! You see, love could not be love unless the persons involved had a choice. God is giving both you and I the choice to listen or not to listen. To harken or not to harken. To obey what is good, or to justify ourselves through the appeal of the devil's lie and make decisions contrary to the life that He has purposed for us.

The result is right before you. BLESSED! It's that simple. You will be blessed when you keep the ways of wisdom. The question is, "What do I get out of serving the Lord? What do I get out of not involving myself in what all my friends or associates seem to be having so much fun in? How do I benefit by going contrary to most of the world"? How, How, How? What, What, What? The questions just never stop coming when your flesh loses control, and your spirit rises up. The bible says,

Notes
_____
_____
_____
_____
_____
_____
_____
_____
_____
_____

"This I say then, Walk in the Spirit (Wisdom) and ye shall not fulfil the lust of the flesh. For the flesh lusteth against the Spirit, and the Spirit against the flesh: and these are contrary the one to the other: so that ye cannot do the things that ye would. But if ye be led of the Spirit (Wisdom), ye are not under the law." Galatians 5:16-18

The bottom line issue is that you must be born again as Jesus told Nicodemus. The world makes light of this because they walk in darkness. It simply means that the real you is awakened through the death and resurrection of Christ. You now begin to live your life based on a wisdom that comes from above (James 3:13-18), and not on the wisdom of the earth that brings destruction, division, pain, and eventually death. Just look at the fruit of what you believe. Are you blessed? What benefit have you gotten from living your life based on your present decision? Come on, face it. I'm not talking about what you feel. I'm talking about what you see. Listen to your conscience. Do you have an assurance that can even face death? Is your life being lived by chance and you just accept whatever happens as truth? In your own way, are you simply running from truth, from God, and from the love that you cannot explain? All this to simply do what you think you want to do rather than submit yourself to a all powerful loving God. My child, listen to me and be blessed.

Notes

APPLICATION

Just begin to put God's truths to the acid test in your life. Speak to Him in the secret place of your heart. Even tell Him if you're mad, or upset at Him for any reason. Put the burden upon God to reveal Himself to you. Just come with a willing heart to listen when He speaks in the way He chooses to speak. In other words, don't tell Him what to do. Just make yourself available by drawing near to Him and then He will draw near to you (James 4:8). Be aware of His peace, for only God can provide peace.

Wisdom:

No other spirit can give you peace but the Lord. As you apply yourself, this peace will continue to prevail over all your fears, and the issues that are facing you. It's a peace that surpasses all understanding. A God that can do that is the only One and true God through Jesus Christ your Lord.

"And the peace of God, which passeth all understanding, shall keep your hearts and minds through Christ Jesus."
Philipians 4:7

Notes
_____
_____
_____
_____
_____
_____
_____
_____
_____
_____
_____

Pro 8:33 Listen to my instruction and be wise; do not ignore it.

Ignorance is a result of intentionally ignoring the truth. To listen means that you just did not hear but you received. Without this receiving, you will not be wise. This is why going to church is not the issue. Those who find their security in going to church alone find themselves still ignorant because they did not receive what they heard. They heard it and somehow argued it out of their life.

There is no getting around the fact that if you want the benefits of being blessed, you have to submit yourself under the mighty hand of God. God is not going to debate His truth with you. There is no compromise with the eternal God Who came in the form of a man, namely Jesus Christ, and gave Himself up for you that you might be reconciled to Him. This is a great and profound mystery which cannot be understood with the facilities of your mere logic. If it could, He would not be Who He is, so He has a right to be submitted to, especially when He proves Himself on your behalf daily that what He is saying is true.

We want to somehow justify our rebellious nature and try to fix it ourselves and that cannot be done. The answer is to listen and be wise. Do not ignore it. It is simple, straight forward, and powerful.

APPLICATION

Why not simply begin? If you have gone this far in the book, it's because you have been given grace by God to accept the truth. You have considered the arguments presented and have compared them to your life as it is. Now you see just how powerful wisdom is. The only through Jesus Christ. I'm not going to suggest that you *try* it. There is nothing else to do but to *DO IT!*

Notes

Say this prayer. "Lord in heaven, here I am. Look upon my life and forgive me of my sins. I admit that I need you to set me free from this law of sin, and to empower me to live in accordance with your wisdom. I believe that You died for my sins and rose from the grave. I confess with my mouth the Lord Jesus Christ, and I expect you to be my God and direct me into all truth. I choose to listen to your instruction from now on, and not to ignore it. I believe that I will be wise and thus be blessed. Amen and Amen.

Wisdom:

If you simply read this prayer, that's okay. But if you want it to be yours, go back and pray this prayer and you will experience the peace and joy that will flood your soul which no religion can ever do. This is relationship with the Son of the Living God. Go ahead.... make His day. He is waiting for you right at the doors of your heart and because these are His words, you can even perceive His presence right now. The bible says, *"No man can come unto me except the Father which has sent me draw him and I will raise him up at the last day." John 6:44.*

Notes

_____
_____
_____
_____
_____
_____
_____
_____
_____
_____
_____

What you feel right now is that drawing of the Holy Spirit upon your heart. Yield to it and live.

Pro 8:34 Blessed is the man who listens to me, watching daily at my doors, waiting at my doorway.

The power to bless rests solely with God. What God has blessed, no man can curse. If you have just received Jesus Christ as your Lord and Savior, you are blessed because you have listened to the extent of responding. Now you must form the important habit of watching daily at the doors of wisdom.

Society is always waiting at someone's doors. There's the psychiatrist, the philosopher, our friend, Tarot cards, the 900 liars who want your money, and even preachers of the gospel who complicate the salvation message and desire to make people followers after them and not after Christ.

The Principle Thing: Get It!

The only door you need to be found watching and waiting at is at the door of wisdom. This means that you will commit yourself to a diligent prayer life and communion with the Lord. This is a daily practice that will insure a blessing in too many ways to comprehend. Don't expect the benefits of serving God to just drop out of the sky. The Kingdom of Heaven doesn't come with observation. It comes from within you. It doesn't take forever either. I notice the benefits of wisdom every minute of my life. And I really notice the results when I choose not to apply myself to wisdom and rather choose a route that was not God's perfect will. However, even this is in the will of God because the bible says,

"And we know that all things work together for good to them that love God, to them who are the called according to his purpose". Romans 8:28.

APPLICATION

Keep this exercise simple by giving the Lord the first minutes of your day. Commit to reading 1 or 2 chapters of Proverbs per day, first thing in the morning if possible. Before you read, simply spend a little time in worshipping the Lord and use Matthew 6:9-16 as a guideline in your prayer. You must invest in your relationship with God or you will get nothing out of it. God has promised that if we seek Him with our whole heart, we will find Him (Jeremiah 29:13). You cannot be deceived by the religious order of the day

Notes

_____

_____

_____

_____

_____

_____

_____

_____

_____

_____

_____

and think all you need is church on Sunday and some religious songs on the radio. You have to have relationship with your Creator in order for Him to have relationship with you.

The result is obvious; Blessed! Your time spent with Him will result in being blessed and walking in a wisdom that will be noticed by people around you. Apply the literal watching at His doors, and remember to wait as well.

Notes
_____
_____
_____
_____
_____
_____
_____
_____
_____
_____
_____
_____

Pro 8:35 For whoever finds me finds life and receives favor from the LORD.

Can you undermine the power of this statement? *"Whoever finds me finds life"*! In addition to this, you will receive favor from the Lord Himself. There is no mistaking this. Whoever tries to justify the truth that God has set forth will do so to their own destruction. There is no discrimination found in this either. He says "whoever" finds me. Black, white, rich, poor, middle class, politician, lawyer; whoever chooses the pathway of the Lord shall find life and be looked upon by God in a favorable way.

People are always found saying, "Well, the Lord understands and He loves everybody". Yes, this is true. The Lord understands so much that He has provided you with the means to understand Him. Those who find Him are those who are looking for Him, not those who deceive themselves into thinking that God is just going to do anything for anybody at anytime. God has an order for every area of our life, and that order is found in the pages of the Holy Bible. If you can't find the order that you have been living by in the word of God, then your order is wrong. This is precisely the reason why things are the way they are in your life.

Jesus said, "*I am the Way, the Truth, and the Life*"...(John 14:6). The life you want is not a list of do's and don'ts. It's not mere proverbs that sound good. True proverbs speak or point to a person, not merely an idea. Your hope is not securing yourself in mere rhetoric about some high and lofty idealism about life. Your hope will be found in the person of Jesus Christ Who is the only Life. This life He promises exceeds mere words. They are words, but they come forth in spirit and in power for godly living. Jesus said it Himself. "*The words that I speak unto you they are spirit and they are life* (John 6:63).

It's in the person of Jesus. Jesus was not One of the prophets pointing to God. He said, "*I and the Father are one and the same*" and "*when you have seen me, you have seen the Father*"(John 10:30, 14:9). Know from this day forward that finding the truth is finding Jesus, and when you do, know that you have not chosen Him but He has chosen you before the foundations of the world (John 15:16; 2 Timothy 1:9).

Notes

_____
_____
_____
_____
_____
_____
_____
_____
_____
_____
_____

Wisdom:

APPLICATION

Determine the consequences you want to have. Go ahead. Do you want the purpose filled marriage? Do you want the fulfillment in life even without being married? Do you want the security that money cannot give, the wealth it cannot impart, the joy that comes from the inside?

Do you want a knowing that mere words cannot express? A shining from your countenance that verifies you belong to God? Expressions of joy and life that feed the people around you, and the ability to stand when the world is against you? Do you want life? Not temporary life. Not the life people think they get from liquor, mere sex, or materialism. But LIFE that can only be given by Jesus the Christ, the Son of the Living God. Repent, and believe, for the Kingdom of God is at hand. Behold It is suddenly upon you. Believe.

Pro 8:36 But whoever fails to find me harms himself; all who hate me love death."

Notes
_____
_____
_____
_____
_____
_____
_____
_____
_____
_____

How much clearer can one be? The conclusion is clear. If you fail to seek after wisdom, no one is hurt but you. You will be the recipient of all the results of failing to obtain wisdom through a diligent search of everything that is within your reach. Even the sky and nature testifies that there is a God. By ignoring the reality of the One True God as Creator of all, you choose to love death. You choose to take the hand of destruction, the path of lifelessness, and many purposeless trials. By forsaking wisdom, you daily bring harm of some form of fashion upon yourself is the conclusion of forsaking wisdom.

Clearly, without a doubt, God is making the point that you will bring harm that results in death upon yourself if you ignore the plea of wisdom. You are moving in the direction of life or the direction of death. You may choose to interpret your own idea of what your consequences are. Through grand persuasion, you might set up a great argument of why the bible is simply ideas and opinion of men and so on. I'm sure you'll even persuade a few people to follow your unfounded philosophy that is merely based on the first lie presented to Eve, namely, *"hath God said"* (Gen. 3:1). However, in the end, your reasons will be found a lie. Even before the end manifests, your daily life will show harm. It will reveal darkness, fear, anxieties, and bondage to sin. You will yet not be free from the entrapment of society.

Notes

_____
_____
_____
_____
_____
_____
_____
_____
_____
_____
_____

Unmistaken evidence that a person is void of relationship with Christ is that they have relationship with people who bring harm to themselves and others. There is an aura of death. This doesn't mean that they look dead, but it means that their direction, their aspirations, communication, and daily orientation is based upon the mere humanistic issues of this life. Naturally, there is a form of godliness, yet, through their very life-style, they deny the power of God.

Wisdom:

Finding the embodiment of wisdom is in the Person of Jesus Christ. 1 Corinthians 1:30 reveals Who Wisdom is by name. It is not Mohammed, Confucius, or any personality whose history dates back to when they were born and ended when they died. Wisdom is revealed through a Person Whose beginning is in Himself. In fact, He is the very END. He is spoken of before He descended to earth through the Immaculate Conception. He was with the Father in the beginning, and when you've seen Him you have seen the Father. He it was Who laid down His life and took it up again. Indeed, I could continue to prove by scripture and history the validity of Jesus Who is Wisdom to us.

Notes

_____
_____
_____
_____
_____
_____
_____
_____
_____
_____
_____

"But of him are ye in Christ Jesus who of God is made unto us wisdom, and righteousness, and sanctification, and redemption:" 1 Cor. 1:30 *Wisdom The Principle Thing: GET IT!*

APPLICATION

Whatever you do from this day forward, do not, I repeat, DO NOT, fail to find Jesus. Stop playing with the years of your youth by thinking that you have time. Every day that you ignore the life that Christ obtained for you through His death and resurrection, you are walking that more closer to death.

Without the simple act of repenting, you will not find Him. When you finish with those highly intellectual arguments, you still must ask the Lord to forgive you of your sins, and to cleanse you from all unrighteousness. When this resounds from the depths of your hurt, and as you continue this attitude of prayer and surrendering, you will be taken higher into His presence.

Why is wisdom the principle thing that you need to get it? Because wisdom is relationship with Jesus Christ and He died to get you!

Face it.
Face yourself. And then Face Jesus.
Face the fact that you are where you are.
Face it.
Face the fact that you are who you are; born in sin. Face yourself. Now...
Face Jesus.
WISDOM!

This is the principle thing.
And I believe you've got it!

Notes

_____
_____
_____
_____
_____
_____
_____
_____
_____
_____
_____

Answer a few questions

What is the most important decision facing you right now?
_____
What verse in Proverbs 8 would begin to help you discover the
answer? _____
Why _____

Would you discribe your friends as wise? _____
What verse in Proverbs 8 best describes your friends?
Why _____

What was your favorite verse? _____
Why? _____

What impact did it have on your life _____
_____

Do you believe you will make your decisions differently after
reading this book? _____

Why? _____

Will you tell someone about wisdom everyday? _____
Will you study proverbs everyday? _____

Discussion or Personal Notes

Discussion or Personal Notes

Read other books by William Owens

Order at www.throughpeople.com

There is an order of men and an order of God. For those who dare to fulfill the mandate of God on their lives, Divine Protocol was written. Divine Protocol is a clarion call to seek the kingdom of God and cease from the traditions of men. It is a revealed word to those who simply desire to move forward in the work of God's kingdom through His Son, Jesus Christ. From the days of John the Baptist until now, the kingdom of heaven suffereth violence and the violent take it by force. Complete dedication to God's kingdom and nothing less is required.

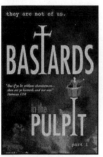

Exposing the problem of bastards in the pulpit is not a choice as servants of God. Rather, it is a mandate, an irrevocable order, a command bearing a weight of responsibility that extends into eternity. It is time for the Body of Christ to boldly identify the difference between one who has been purged from self-interests, political agendas, fear of faces, and hidden sins, even to one who justifies his sins because of grace. In these days of increasing apostasy, we must realize there are sons and then there are bastards…in the pulpit.

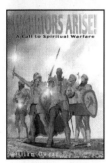

The purpose of this book is to point you to the power of God's Word within you. If you do not have God's governing authority working through you to bring about His will in the earth, any hope that you possess will be quickly swept away by this forthcoming conflict. This conflict is manifesting itself increasingly within the natural realm and encroaching upon our society at an alarming rate. War, famine, strange weather patterns, crimes of all kinds, and senseless murder abound. These are signs of the times, and the only effective and relevant place to be is waging a good war!   *www.warriorsarise.org*

Naked before God – words that express my heart, is a compilation of poems written during the contemplative times of when William stands before God. During these sacred moments, he unashamedly bares his heart before God and exposes himself to the unfathomable grace, love and understanding that God is so willing to show him. Suddenly – words that express his heart begin to flow! You will be blessed as you grasp the depth, yet simplicity, of these words. While many of these poems are borne out of William's own experience, others are written after reflection upon the lives of both biblical characters and people that have cross his path.   *www.nakedbeforeGod.com*